How to Get a **Fair Trial** by Jury

How to Get a Fair Trial by Jury

Picking the Jury in a Criminal Case

Second Edition

By RANDOLPH JACKSON

WE THE PEOPLE PRESS
Brooklyn, New York

WE THE PEOPLE PRESS
PO Box 23405
Brooklyn, NY 11202-3405
www.randolphjackson.com

ISBN-10 0-9795946-1-8
ISBN-13 978-0-9795946-1-8

Copyright © 1978, 2003 by Randolph Jackson

All rights to this material, including, without limitation;
rights to reproduction or use thereof in any form, are
expressly reserved.

First edition published 1978.
Second edition published in 2003. Reprinted in 2010.

Library of Congress Control Number: 2010928481

DESIGNED BY CHERYL HANNA
EDITED BY GEOFFREY JACQUES
IMAGES & ILLUMINATIONS
www.imagesandilluminations.com

For RATHENIA

CONTENTS

About the Author

Justice Randolph Jackson was born in Bedford Stuyvesant, Brooklyn, New York. He is a graduate of Stuyvesant High School, New York University and Brooklyn Law School.

After working in the Wall Street firm of Nixon, Mudge, Rose, Guthrie, Alexander & Mitchell, (former President Richard Nixon's firm), Justice Jackson engaged in numerous community service, legal and charitable activities. He served as a Housing Court Judge, a Civil Court Judge, and a Criminal Court Judge before his election to a fourteen-year term as a Justice of the Supreme Court of the State of New York. He was re-elected in 2002 to a second consecutive fourteen-year term on the Supreme Court. Justice Jackson was formerly a commissioned officer in the New York State Guard, serving with the rank of Lieutenant Colonel. He serves as a mentor to inner-city youth. He is a life member of the NAACP and the National Bar Association. He is an author, Bible teacher, empowerment consultant, motivational speaker, and patron of the arts.

His first book, *How to Get a Fair Trial by Jury,* was published in 1978. It has been extensively revised for this edition. His second book, *Black People in the Bible,* was published in 2002 by Vantage Press (New York). It is available online at www.blackpeopleinthebible.com, www.amazon.com, www.barnesandnoble.com, or from the publisher, Vantage Press.

How to Get a Fair Trial by Jury

Introduction

A lawyer can bring tears to the eyes of spectators with a summation to the jury. He or she can destroy witnesses by a withering cross-examination. He or she can present fifteen character witnesses to establish the defendant's towering reputation in the community. But if the jury was not selected properly, if the prejudice which the jurors brought with them into the courtroom was not dealt with in a professional manner, all the lawyer's work will be in vain and that jury will vote guilty.

The most important part of a jury trial is the jury. It follows, then, that selecting the jury is the lawyer's most important job.

The jury must be swept clean of individuals with bias against the defendant or the defendant's case. There are some individuals who are ready to vote guilty as soon as they see the defendant or as soon as they hear the charges.

An obvious example is a woman who has been the victim of a rape and who is now called upon to serve as a juror in a rape case. Or a member of the Klu Klux Klan where the defendant is an African American. Or a policeman assigned to the narcotics squad when the charge is the sale of narcotics.

The remaining jurors must be educated to the defendant's point of view. They must be made aware of the issues that will be raised by the defense, the points that will be established by cross-examination of prosecution witnesses, and, fundamentally, why they should vote not guilty in spite of the charges that have been brought against the defendant.

If these things are done well, and a good jury obtained, the jurors will excuse weaknesses in the defense case and will pounce upon weakness in the prosecution's case. They will look for a reason to acquit the defendant and they will resist pressures to convict. Since the ultimate decision is in the hands of the members of the jury, the lawyer must be sure that the jury is well selected.

If the lawyer does his job well in the selection process, the defendant must get a fair trial. If the job is not done well, if bias and prejudice are allowed to enter the trial through the jury, the defendant cannot get a fair trial.

The purpose of this book is to explain clearly and simply how to obtain a fair trial through the jury selection process.

These words about jury selection factors and techniques apply equally to civil trials.

Purposes of Voir Dire

In the hands of a skilled lawyer the jury selection or voir dire process has many purposes. It is far easier to know what to ask the jurors if you know why you are asking questions.

Perhaps the most obvious purpose is to *eliminate* from the jury all persons whose attitude is such that they are sure to vote guilty no matter what the evidence. Some persons have such respect for the government that they feel if the government or one of its agencies says the defendant is guilty, then it must be so. Others perceive it as their duty to help the government by convicting an accused person.

There are people who believe that all persons of a particular background have a propensity to commit crime and must be guilty if charged. The facts of a particular crime may be so heinous in the eyes of a particular juror that anyone accused of it will be looked at with revulsion.

All persons who are obviously biased against the defense must be removed from the panel.

A second major purpose of voir dire is to *inform*

those who will be selected to serve just what your case is about. They already know that the defendant is charged with the sale of drugs. They are curious and want to know more.

A skillful lawyer will satisfy that curiosity and help his or her case by letting them know that the defendant will claim that he is a victim of mistaken identity, or that he was only an innocent bystander, or that he was duped and entrapped by improper, over-reaching police tactics.

Thus, the jury is immediately advised of the other side of the case and does not have to go for days or weeks knowing only that the defendant is or may be a drug seller.

Another purpose for which some lawyers employ the voir dire is to *purge* weak aspects of their cases. If the defendant will not testify, or will testify but has a criminal record, the lawyer may let drop some hints of this during voir dire so as to remove the shock effect of this information when it is disclosed at a later point. A further purpose is to find out if any members of the jury are so affected by this fact that they cannot be impartial.

Voir Dire Techniques for Lawyers

The courtroom is a stage and our trial is a drama in which the lawyer should be at once the director and a leading character.

When a panel of prospective jurors is brought into the courtroom they know very little of what is about to happen and nothing about the case.

The lawyer's job is to educate them. To do this, their attention must be gained and held. A bit of intimidation also helps. Effective attention-getting techniques include varying the modulation of the voice (selective shouting), speaking so everyone can hear, standing as close as possible to the person being questioned; staring at the person being spoken to and asking questions that are short and easy to understand and that have an obvious reason.

Speaking in a monotone is to be avoided. You can gain attention by the way in which you speak. You should speak to everyone in the room. If you hold a *private* conversation with the person to whom you are speaking, everyone else will lose interest or fall asleep.

You should stand close to the person you are talking to. Standing far away establishes an emotional distance as well as a physical one. You want them *involved* with you and your case, not detached.

Many lawyers *read* their questions. However, any impact which such questions may have is thus dissipated. You should look at the person to whom you are speaking.

The jury should be able to understand what you are doing. They may not be able to follow what the other lawyer and the judge are doing or understand the procedures in the court. If they can see your purpose and follow your actions, they will take a greater interest in your case. The more interested they are, the more likely they are to adopt your reasoning.

The lawyer should from the outset *take* the attention of the jury and keep it on himself or herself. How many times have you seen jurors half asleep and inattentive while the other lawyer drones on with his repetitive, pointless questions?

Everyone should sit up a little straighter when the good lawyer rises to speak. No one should be bored by your questions. Ask a few routine information-gathering questions of the panel as a whole.

["How many of you are in your last week of jury duty and would be unable to continue if this trial lasts past Friday?"]

Then plunge right in and attack the person you would most like to eliminate. Never go in line from number one straight through to the end. This is likely to induce terminal narcolepsy. You know whom you don't want. Go after them. Hit them with all your bombshells and subtle tricks at the very beginning of the day. Let everyone else in the room know what's waiting for them if they have even a trace of bias against your client or his case. Establish a moral tone so that when your remaining challenges are few, it won't matter because the jurors will eliminate themselves.

If you have done this well, you'll find unwanted jurors spontaneously telling the judge, "I don't think I can be fair."

Bias is deep-seated, not easily exposed to public view. You must be an artist to induce the jurors to admit or show their bias. Do not be afraid to antagonize a juror. A likely candidate is one whom you know you will eliminate anyway. Tear into him. ["You have no friends like the defendant?" "You have no neighbors like him?" "You have no club members like him?" "What is there in your background that would lead you to believe that you can be fair to this defendant?]

CATEGORIES OF VOIR DIRE QUESTIONS

The questions the lawyer will ask in voir dire fall into certain categories.

First, you are seeking to determine if the juror meets minimal qualifications required by law. ["How old are you?"] Some may be disqualified by age.

Second, you want general facts about the prospective juror, which will assist you in deciding to keep him or reject him.

["Where were you born?" "What neighborhood do you live in?"]

Third, you want to discover the juror's general attitudes and personality.

["What magazines do you read?" "What clubs do you belong to?" "Have you or a close relative ever been the victim of a violent crime?"]

Fourth, you want to know if the juror may be prejudiced against your client because of religion, race, sex, national origin, age or for any other reason.

The purpose of voir dire is to enable the lawyer to

obtain hints of prejudice and to develop evidence of prejudice by a series of questions.

Suppose your client is a Chicano accused of a crime. Obviously few people seated in a crowded courtroom will admit forthrightly before fifty witnesses that they don't like Chicanos.

["Do you have any Chicano neighbors?"

"Do you have any Chicano friends?"

"Do you belong to any clubs or organizations with Chicano members?"

"Do you feel that Chicanos tend to commit more crimes than other people?"]

Fifth, you want to know the jurors' attitudes about crucial points of law such as the presumption of innocence and the prosecutors burden to prove guilt beyond a reasonable doubt.

["Do you feel the defendant has to prove his innocence?"] "Yes", many will answer, even after being instructed to the contrary by the judge.

See Appendix "A" for a full set of suggested voir dire questions, intended as a guideline only. Other questions will suggest themselves to you as each situation develops.

This set of questions will come in handy in Federal Court, where the attorney is usually not permitted to question the jurors. Simply type out all your questions under the heading: *Proposed Voir Dire on Behalf of Defendant "X"* and submit them to the judge in advance.

You may also choose to advise the judge of the special circumstances of your case which require that the *attorneys* question the jurors, as provided by Rule 24(a) of the Federal Rules of Criminal Procedure.

Whom to Accept

General guidelines can be set down, but they must be flexible, not ironclad.

Every case is unique. Generally speaking, you are looking for someone who will react favorably to the defendant or his case.

What sorts of people may be expected to react in this way?

It is a crime in America to be poor, to be a loser. Yet there is a cross current of feeling for an underdog who puts up a good fight.

Your client is an underdog. The power and force of the Government are arrayed against him. You want jurors who understand what it is to be an underdog and who can feel for the underdog.

Among what groups are you more likely to find such persons?

Blacks, Hispanics, homosexuals, young people, persons with relatives who have been convicted of crime, persons who have themselves been convicted of crime, persons with a physical disability, Jews: anyone who knows what it is like to be persecuted, discriminated against, kicked in the face.

Of course, not everyone reacts equally to bad treatment. Some adopt the mannerisms of the oppressor and develop a harsh attitude against underdogs. These are easily spotted by their uptight, artificial behavior.

Evaluating the Juror

Whom to Reject

Our job is to reject those who don't fit and to educate those who remain. Most jurors are *not* selected.

They don't pass. The system is really jury *rejection* rather than jury selection.

How and why do we reject?

1. Neighborhood
2. Face
3. Previously Convicted
4. Volunteer
5. Age
6. Prosecution Witnesses
7. Relatives
8. Occupation
9. Supervisor
10. Nationality

1.   Neighborhood

In your town, I'm sure people from a certain neighborhood are well-known for not liking people from a certain other neighborhood. If the prospective juror comes from the neighborhood known to be antagonistic to your client's part of town, watch out! Not everyone from that neighborhood is an automatic guilty vote, but be careful.

I keep on my table during jury selection a map of the town. I ask every juror for his or her zip code to pinpoint their neighborhood. I want to make sure I am getting a cross-section of the community and not an overload from the wrong neighborhood. If the count is wrong I pointedly let the jury know that my client is not getting a fair break ["Congratulations Mrs. Moore, you are the 6th person from Junction Flat to be selected for questioning. Did you all come down together?"].

2.   Face

When the juror's name is called and she comes forward to be seated, I place an "X" or a check next to their name. "X" marks an unpleasant, sour, negative face, denoting a probable guilty vote. Check means a pleasant or neutral face which is worth further investigation. Many other reasons for rejection may be present but a bad face is usually a shortcut to spotting them.

Trying a case before a jury full of pleasant faces can become a love affair.

3.   Previously Convicted

Habits are hard to break. When a juror has convicted before, I don't want him on my jury. You can't ask him if he's voted guilty but you can ask if he's served on a jury. ["What were the charges? Were you the foreman? Did you reach a verdict? How long did you deliberate? Were you satisfied with your verdict?"] It's not hard to guess if he's convicted before. If he has, let him go. Don't give him a chance to use his experience and "superior" knowledge of the law to convince the other jurors to vote guilty.

4.   Volunteer

["Were you subpoenaed or did you volunteer for jury duty?]

Beware the court buff that's served so many times

he can't remember them all.

For most citizens, jury duty is a rare, and perhaps an inconvenient experience. Watch out for the juror who likes jury duty and who has volunteered. I seldom waive a jury trial because the average judge has seen so many guilty persons come before him, he or she thinks they're all guilty. So, too, does the sophisticated, veteran juror. Give me a new face, virgin territory on which to make a fresh impression.

5.   AGE

["How old are you?"]

Call me prejudiced but young people tend to be better jurors for the defendant. An elderly person is more likely to be too set in his or her ways to put aside the bias we all have and give the defendant the benefit of the doubt.

This is not to deny that there are many good jurors of advanced age whom you very much want to select. But, all other things being equal, of two unattractive jurors, I'll choose to be stuck with the younger one on the chance he might respond better to the challenge I'm going to put before him.

6.   Prosecution Witnesses

Select the jury with the background of the prosecution witnesses in mind. If the major prosecution witness is a Hungarian, I don't want five Hungarian jurors sitting there, watching me tear apart their countryman, sympathizing with him all the way. I have nothing against Hungarians in any trial, except this one.

7.   Juror's Relatives

["Where does your spouse work? Where did your spouse work before retirement?"]

The juror may be fine but his spouse may work for the FBI. This may make for an unexpected adverse verdict if you're in Federal Court and the principal prosecution witnesses are FBI agents.

8. Occupation

["Where do you work and what do you do?"]

Don't put your life and liberty into the hands of the fellow who forecloses on mortgages, the guy who adjusts claims for an insurance company, the one who handles collections for a utility, or the lady who investigates fraudulent businessmen. Like the jurors with extensive prior jury service, they have heard all the excuses, all the stories, all the defenses. They have found them lacking. They are liable to find your defense lacking. They may not even need to leave the jury box to decide on a guilty verdict. Let them sit on someone else's case.

9. Supervisor

["How many people, if any, do you supervise in your work?"] Occasionally, despite your vigilance, a bad juror will be sworn in. Make sure that person is not also a commanding leader, accustomed to giving orders to 50 people every day. Supervisors are not bad if they are in your corner, but a bad juror who is also a supervisor can be dangerous. He or she will not be persuaded by the other jurors and may persuade them.

10. Nationality

["Where were you born and where were your parents born?"]

Some countries have a long history of affording no

civil liberties to their citizens. People from those countries may tend to assume that an individual involved in a dispute against the government is automatically wrong.. On the other hand, some countries have a tradition of steadfastly resisting armies of occupation. Someone from such a country may sympathize with an underdog, such as your client and may be skeptical of authority, including the prosecutor's.

I like the point system in jury rejection, also known as "the three strikes and you're out" system. A person with a bad face from the wrong *neighborhood* who has *convicted* before is an automatic rejection.

An *elderly volunteer* whose *background* parallels the main prosecution witness is also out.

THE HIGHEST ART

The Successful Challenge for Cause

You have now decided that the juror before you must not be allowed to sit on this case. The question arises, how do you get him off? He has steadfastly resisted all of your invitations to take himself off, despite the moral tone you have created. You don't want to use up your remaining peremptory challenge on him, because what's left in the jury panel looks even worse.

Now is the time to pull out your trump card, the challenge for cause. Somehow, you must get the juror to admit to a state of mind which would prevent him from giving the defendant a fair trial.

The Voir Dire in this instance becomes a form of cross-examination, with the objective of getting the "witness" to commit himself to a disqualifying statement.

You will lead the juror up a blind alley from which there is no retreat or ramble through an innocuous line and suddenly switch to a devastating attack. Let us suppose the juror is married to a policeman.

The normal question, [Would the fact that your husband is a police officer prevent you in any way from rendering a fair and impartial verdict in this case?] , will bring forth the normal answer, [No!] Instead explore what it means to be married to a cop.

[What hours does your husband work?

Does that mean you are asleep when he comes home? Do you ever wake up when he should have gotten home and find him not there?

Do you worry about his safety when he is at work? Has he ever been hurt on the job?

Have any of his friends been hurt on the job? Does your husband have any cases pending with the prosecutor's office? Isn't he working in close connection with the prosecutor's office right now?

Do you know if the prosecutor handling this case is one of those he is working with now?

Do your husband's co-workers visit your home? Do you visit the homes of your husband's fellow police officers? How often?

Do you have respect for your husband's job?

Don't you believe that policemen generally tell the truth? Wouldn't you tend to believe the testimony of a police officer more than the testimony of a person accused of a crime?

Mrs. Smith, you are married to a policeman and you socialize with policemen on a regular basis. The testimony of police officers will be a crucial part of this case.

Don't you feel it would be unfair to the defendant for a person in your position to sit on this case?

Don't you think the fact of your close contact with police officers in general and with one police officer in particular might give you a different perspective on the case from the other jurors?]

A side-effect of these questions, aside from eliciting a disqualifying statement from the juror, will be to impress upon all the remaining jurors the importance of being fair to the defendant.

Every good lawyer will develop in his or her arsenal a question or two to fit a particular situation. If the juror looks doubtful and is a Hasidic Jew, ask him: [If there were a conflict between the law of this state as explained to you by the judge and the law of the Talmud, which law would you follow?].

If the juror looks like a definite guilty vote but has not committed himself, ask him: [Does the defendant have to prove to you he is innocent?].

Note the importance of having a juror who is naive and unsophisticated, and who is hearing the questions for the first time. A veteran juror, having heard it all before, will tailor his or her answers to make himself acceptable.

Out-Foxing the Prosecutor

How can you get the prosecutor to eliminate someone you don't want or to accept someone you do want? With a little psychological massage.

Let us suppose the juror in question is a *fifty*-year-old lady with a rather *sour* face who's a clerk for a company that *repossesses* cars. By our criteria, she's got three strikes against her and we don't want her. But why use up a peremptory challenge if we can get the prosecutor to eliminate her for us? Try to show that you have some personal bond with that juror.

[Where were you born? Is that near__________?

What company do you work for? Do you know__________, __________ or__________?]

The nervous prosecutor, afraid of your getting a friendly juror, will challenge the person you didn't want anyway.

Suppose the defendant is Hispanic and you expect prosecutor to find all Hispanic jurors somehow unsuitable. Start the first time the prosecutor peremptorily kicks a Hispanic off the jury. Ask for a conference at side-bar and tell the judge your client is not getting a fair trial because:

1. He is entitled to be tried by a jury of his peers. If all Hispanics are systematically excluded, the defendant's constitutional rights to a trial by his peers are being violated.

2. The rights of the Hispanic jurors on the panel to serve on jury duty and to participate equally with Whites in the process of jury trials are also being violated by the prosecutor's intentional exclusion of Hispanics. See *Strauder vs. West Virginia*, 100 U.S. 303 (1880); *U.S. vs. Robinson*, 45 USLW 2216 (USDC, Conn 1976), *rev'd* ____F.2d____(2d Cir. 1977) and *People vs. Wheeler*, 47 USLW 2264 (Calif. Sup. Ct, 9-25-78).

Record the name of each Hispanic excluded by the prosecutor. Periodically state for the record, "The prosecutor has now exercised five of his nine challenges, or 55% exclusively against Hispanics; specifically Mr. ________, Mrs. ________ and Miss________. Keep hammering into the judge, the prosecutor and the record on appeal, the fact that the prosecutor's actions are preventing your client from getting a fair trial. Notwithstanding the denial of all your motions and the prosecutor's protestations of being colorblind, you will find more Hispanics being allowed on the jury, which is, after all, your object.

What to Do When the Deck Is Stacked Against You

The Challenge to the Array

Sometimes you will know from previous experience that the panel of prospective jurors will be seriously deficient in female, minority, young or some other category of jurors crucial to your defense. In other words, the jury clerk has stacked the deck against you by eliminating in advance all or most of a certain type of juror.

Certain counties are notorious for substantial under-representation of certain ethnic and other groups on jury panels. You should never handle a case in such a county without making a written challenge to the composition of the jury panel.

Your motion should set forth the particulars of the unfair condition. You must state in your papers what group is under-represented or excluded in the jury panel. You should also state the mechanism, if known, which created the under-representation. For example, perhaps a statute permitted women to claim an exemption from jury duty solely on the basis of sex.

Any statistical or documentary evidence which you have should be included in your papers.

See Appendix B for a sample "Challenge to the Jury Panel."

Alternate Jurors

After selecting the members of the jury, it is customary to select alternate jurors who will serve in the event a juror is forced to leave the case during the trial. Many lawyers tend to relax their standards when the time comes to select alternates, and understandably so. Jury selection is tedious, tiresome work.

The feeling is, "We've got a good jury. The alternates don't count, it won't matter if this *loser* is sworn as an alternate. He can't hurt us."

Don't fall into this trap. Don't let up when selecting alternates. They frequently end up deliberating and voting. They can hurt you, even if they are excused at the end of the trial and do not vote. Many jurors eat lunch together, ride home together, and, yes, talk about the case with each other. Do you want a rotten apple poisoning your jury daily for a solid two weeks?

CONCLUSION

I hope my faithful reader has gained something worthwhile from this discussion of the details of the jury selection process and that the techniques suggested to obtain a fair trial through the jury selection process will be helpful. These words about jury selection factors and techniques apply equally to civil trials.

Now that you know how to get a fair trial by jury, go forth and conquer!

—Randolph Jackson

Appendix A

Sample Voir Dire Questions

The defendant and the attorneys have already been identified to you. Is there any of you who knows either the defendant or any of the attorneys? Do you know them personally or do you recognize their names?

Among the witnesses who may be called by the prosecution in this case are the following, and I caution you that my mentioning the names imposes no burden on the prosecution to call that person as a witness:

____

____

____

____

____

Are there any of you who know any of these people?

Does anybody on the jury know anything about this case? Have you witnessed anything which might be related to this case or have you heard or read anything at all about it, either from friends or relatives or from newspapers, magazines, radio or television or otherwise?

Do any of you, or does anyone close to you, such as a friend or relative, work for a law enforcement agency such as the Police Department, the District Attorney's office or any federal law enforcement agency; or have you or anyone close to you done such work in the past? Do any of you have any business pending before the District Attorney's office or the Police Department or some other such agency?

Do any of you or does anyone close to you work for a lawyer or a group principally concerned with law, either as a paid employee or a volunteer, or have you or they done such work in the past?

Has anyone on the jury, or anyone in your family, been the victim of a crime, witnessed a crime or in any way participated in a criminal proceeding?

How many days have you been on jury duty? Been questioned in other cases? Have you been excused in other courtrooms? Do you know why you were excused?

Have any of you ever served on a jury in a criminal or civil case before?

In your previous jury service, what type of case was it? What was the charge? How many hours did the jury deliberate? What was the name of the judge? Were you the foreperson? Was a verdict reached?

What neighborhood do you live in? What is your zip code?

How do you spell your name?

What is your place of birth and that of your parents?

What is your marital status?

What is your date of birth?

What is the highest grade in school you completed?

How would you feel if you were black and you were on trial for your liberty and the prosecutor wouldn't let any blacks sit on the jury?

What are your hobbies?

What clubs, associations do you belong to? What offices do you hold in them?

What is your occupation or former occupation (if retired) and that of your spouse?

How many people, if any, do you supervise in your job?

Did you serve in the military? If so, state the dates of service, branch, highest rank achieved and general duties.

In your military service, did you ever serve on courts-martial, military police or shore patrol?

Have you or anyone in your family ever been arrested? If so, please give all details.

If the jury was split eleven to one, and you were the one, how would you feel?

Do you believe there are good and bad law officers just as there are good and bad people?

What newspapers and magazines do you read regularly?

Who is the greatest American of the last century?

What are your views on the question of capital punishment?

How do you feel about the use of cocaine?

What, if any, weapons for self-defense do you keep in your home?

If you were not convinced beyond a reasonable doubt of the defendant's guilt, would you be afraid to march back into this courtroom and announce a verdict of not guilty?

Would you like to sit on this particular case? If so, why?

Do you have any black co-workers?

In your previous criminal jury service, were any of the defendants black?

Do you feel black people by and large have the same opportunity in America as whites?

Do you know what white racism is?

Do you feel that there is white racism in America?

Do you belong to any clubs or organizations that have black members? What are the names of the organizations?

Are you willing to accept the fact that America has been a racist society? Do you agree that we are all products of a racist society? Agents of a racist society?

Do you have any friends who are black?

Do you have any neighbors who are black?

All other things being equal, how do you feel about the reliability of the testimony of a white law enforcement officer as opposed to that of a black person?

Do you feel that blacks tend to commit more crimes than other people?

Would you give more weight to the testimony of a white person than you would the testimony of a black person?

Wouldn't the fact that the defendant is black prevent you from rendering a fair and impartial verdict in this case?

If __________ were to testify, would you take the attitude that "He is liable to say anything because he is on trial for his liberty, and I am not going to believe him"?

What are your feelings on __________'s guilt or innocence? How do you see him now?

If selected for this jury would you feel any obligation to find __________ guilty of *something* if you felt he wasn't guilty of the main charge?

If you are selected, will you base your decision on the *lack* of evidence, as well as the evidence presented?

Do you feel he's probably guilty of *something* because he has been arrested, indicted by a grand jury and brought to trial?

Do you know that in a civil case the plaintiff need only tip the scales in his favor to win, but in a criminal case the prosecution must prove the defendant guilty beyond a reasonable doubt?

If you have a doubt, based upon a reason, as to __________'s guilt, will you vote not guilty?

Do you feel that __________ has to prove he is innocent?

Is it running in your mind right now that this man might be a menace to society?

Do you *really* believe, as he sits here right now, that he

is innocent of any wrongdoing of any kind?

If you were asked to vote right now, guilty or not guilty and all you knew about the case is what you know right now, how would you vote?

Would you vote guilty if you *suspected* was guilty but the evidence was not there?

If a juror for whatever reason were to start out in favor of the prosecution, would you agree that it would not be fair to __________.

Please look at __________. Do you see him as innocent?

Assuming that somebody you love were standing trial in place of __________ for the same crime, would you feel satisfied with 12 jurors who felt the same way as you do now?

Has anything asked the other jurors triggered off something in the crevices of your mind that you would like to tell me about?

Do you know of any reason why it might be inappropriate for you to serve on this case?

What would you do if the judge's instructions went against your grain?

Did anyone here volunteer for jury duty?

Don't you think that the fact that __________ might give you a different perspective on this from the other jurors?

Don't you think it might give __________ the benefit of the doubt if you sat on a different case than this one?

Do you feel any obligation to assist the prosecutor in his or her work on this case?

What are your feelings on police entrapment tactics?

APPENDIX B

*Sample Challenge to the Composition
of the Jury Panel*

(1) COURT

COUNTY OF (2)

————————————————————————————x

THE PEOPLE OF THE STATE OF (:

                          Plaintiff,   :

Docket # (5)

           -against-   :

(4)   :

                       Defendant :

————————————————————————————x.

CHALLENGE TO JURY PANEL

The above-named defendant hereby challenges, pursuant to Criminal Procedure Law (6) the panel of petit jurors drawn for the present term of the (1) Court, County of (2) on the grounds that the pool from which the panel was drawn, and the resulting panel itself, do not represent a fair cross-section of the community in that:

1. Black and Puerto Rican citizens are grossly under-

represented therein; Residents of the neighborhoods represented by the following zip codes are grossly under-represented therein; 11205, 11208, 11212, 11213, 11217, 11221, 11222, 11225, 11227, 11232, 11233, 11237 and;

2.   Residents of the neighborhoods represented by the following zip codes are grossly over-represented: 11229, 11223, 11218, 11214, 11234, all in violation of the defendant's rights under the Sixth and Fourteenth Amendments to the United States Constitution and Judiciary Law, Section 500.

Dated: Brooklyn, New York.

(7)

Yours, etc.,

(8)

Attorneys for Defendant

(9) Address & Telephone #

(1) COURT

COUNTY OF (2)

————————————————————————x

THE PEOPLE OF THE STATE OF (3)   :
AFFIRMATION

                      Plaintiff,   :

Docket # (5)

             -against-   :

(4)   :

                 Defendant   :

————————————————————————x

STATE OF NEW YORK)

COUNTY OF KINGS   )

(6) , Esq., an attorney admitted to practice in the Courts of the State of   (3)   and the attorney for defendant,

(4) , hereby affirms the following to be true under penalty of perjury, except as to the matters herein stated to be alleged on information and belief, and as to those matters, he or she believes them to be true:

1. I am familiar with all the facts and proceedings herein.. I make this affirmation in support of the challenge to the panel by defendant   (4).

2. The defendant, who is black, alleges that African-Americans, residing in substantial numbers in (2)   County, are not fairly represented both on the panel and on the pool from which the panel was drawn. He further alleges that Hispanic Americans are not fairly represented on the panel and the pool.

3. According to the 1970 census, there were 2,602,002 residents of Brooklyn of which 656,194 were black and 392,575 were Hispanic. Thus it can be seen that blacks and Hispanics comprised 40% of the population of Kings County in 1970. If in fact the panel of jurors is drawn at random from the general population, then approximately 40% of the jurors should be black and Hispanic. Such, however, is not the case, in direct violation of the law of this state as expressed in Section 500 of the Judiciary Law, to wit:

> "It is the policy of this state that all litigants in the courts of this state entitled to trial by jury shall have the right to grand and petit juries selected at random from a fair cross-section of the community in the county or other governmental subdivision wherein the court convenes; and that all eligible citizens shall have the opportunity to serve on grand and

petit juries in the courts of this state, and shall have an obligation to serve when summoned for that purpose, unless exempted, disqualified or excused.

4.   The jury panel is supposed to represent a cross-section of the county. If this mandate were carried out, then every community and neighborhood would be represented in approximately equal numbers, In fact, however, neighborhoods from which blacks and Hispanics are excluded, such as Sheepshead Bay, Bay Ridge and Bensonhurst, are statistically significantly over-represented. Neighborhoods in which blacks and Hispanics predominate such as Brownsville, Williamsburg and Bedford Stuyvesant, are either not represented at all or significantly under-represented.

This is a flagrant violation of Judiciary Law, Section 500.

5.   The County Jury Board intentionally does not include a fair cross-section of the community by deliberately failing to utilize lists of utility subscribers, licensed operators of motor vehicles and state and local taxpayers, as provided for in Judiciary Law, Section 506, to wit:

"The commissioner of jurors shall

cause the names of prospective jurors to be selected at random from the voter registration lists, and from such other available lists of the residents of the county as the appropriate appellate division shall specify, such as lists of utility subscribers, licensed operators of motor vehicles, registered owners of motor vehicles, state and local taxpayers, and persons who have volunteered to serve as jurors by filing with the commissioner their names and places of residence."

6. The presentation of a bare prima facie case requires the introduction into evidence of statistics that would tend to demonstrate that there is a disparity over a significant period of time between the demographic composition of the community and the compositions of the pool from which persons are chosen for jury service.

In *Castenada vs. Partida*, 51 L. Ed. 2d 498 (1977), counsel for the defendant demonstrated the existence of significant disparity between the percentage of Mexican-Americans on the Jury List and their relative numbers in the community by comparing the percentage of Spanish surnames on the list against the percentage of Mexican-Americans residing in Hidalgo County, Texas. The population figures and their ethnic composition were obtained from a census study conducted by the Federal Government.

The United States Department of Labor, Immigration and Naturalization Service, has published a pamphlet of Spanish surnames which can be used to identify Spanish surnamed persons on the Jury List.

While Hispanic-Americans may be identified by their surnames, African-Americans cannot. Consequently, a study of black representation in the jury pool can be conducted only if the residence addresses of persons on the List are given, so that the percentage of names from predominantly black neighborhoods can be measured against the percentage of names on the List from non-black or predominantly white neighborhoods.

WHEREFORE, affirmant respectfully requests that this Court allow this challenge to the panel, discharge the panel, and order that a panel of prospective trial jurors in which black and Puerto Rican citizens are represented according to their numbers in the general population be returned for the term.

Dated: Brooklyn, New York

    (7)

____

(6)

Licensing Agreement for eBook Edition

By downloading these files you agree to the terms and conditions in the licensing agreement.

When you purchase an electronic book from We the People Press you are granted a individual license for use of the book for your personal use only. You can make a copy for work and a copy for home use. Please do not share it with friends, colleagues, or strangers.

Anyone who has legal access to the book has the right to print out copies for their own use. But they may not print out copies for use by those without legal access.

Contact We the People Press for information about site and school licenses.

Under no circumstances may copies of the electronic file be made available on public web sites, FTP sites, mailing lists, or by any other publicly accessible means.

Sorry, but no refunds are possible for downloadable online books and papers. Please be sure of your purchases before buying.

www.ingramcontent.com/pod-product-compliance
Lightning Source LLC
Chambersburg PA
CBHW030829060726
47590CB00004B/1464